spot

OCEAN ANIMALS

EELS

by Mari Schuh

AMICUS | AMICUS INK

mouth

skin

Look for these words and pictures as you read.

eye

markings

What is in the sea?
An eel!

Eels are fish.
They look like snakes.

Look at the mouth.

It is open.

This helps eels breathe.

mouth

Look at the skin.

It is smooth.

Most eels do not have scales.

skin

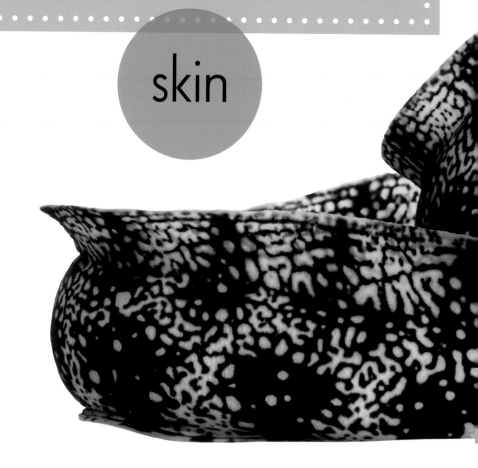

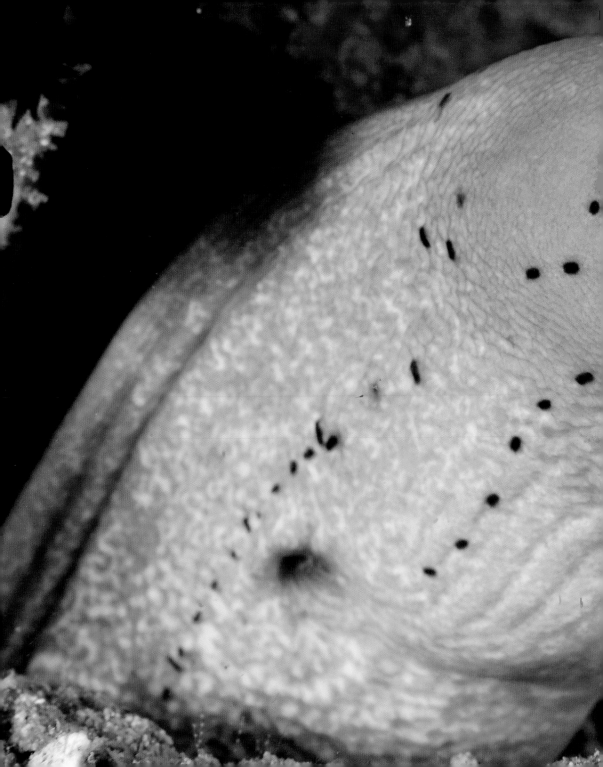

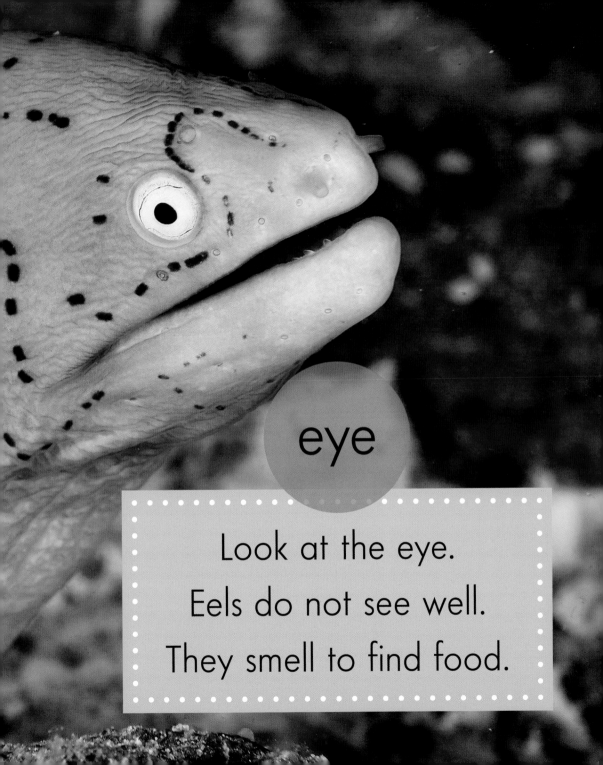

eye

Look at the eye.
Eels do not see well.
They smell to find food.

markings

Look at the markings.
These eels blend in.
Sharks can't see them.

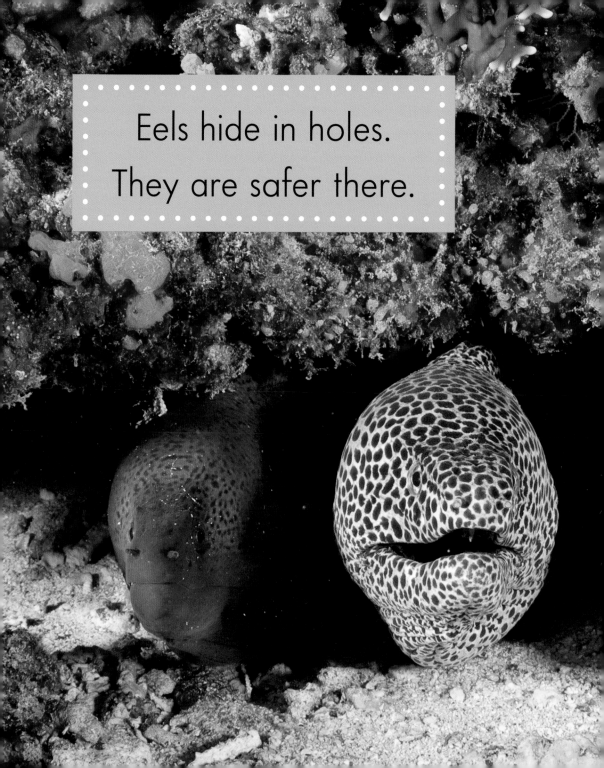

Eels hide in holes.
They are safer there.

mouth

skin

Did you find?

eye

markings

Spot is published by Amicus and Amicus Ink
P.O. Box 1329, Mankato, MN 56002
www.amicuspublishing.us

Library of Congress Cataloging-in-Publication Data
Names: Schuh, Mari C., 1975- author.
Title: Eels / by Mari Schuh.
Description: Mankato, MN : Amicus, [2021] | Series:
  Ocean animals | Audience: Ages 4-7 | Audience:
  Grades K-1
Identifiers: LCCN 2019047388 (print) | LCCN 2019047389
  (ebook) | ISBN 9781645491101 (library binding) | ISBN
  9781681526775 (paperback) | ISBN 9781645491521 (pdf)
Subjects: LCSH: Eels—Juvenile literature.
Classification: LCC QL637.9.A5 S38 2021 (print) | LCC
  QL637.9.A5 (ebook) | DDC 597/.43—dc23
LC record available at https://lccn.loc.gov/2019047388
LC ebook record available at https://lccn.loc.gov/2019047389

Printed in the United States of America

HC   10 9 8 7 6 5 4 3 2 1
PB   10 9 8 7 6 5 4 3 2 1

Alissa Thielges, editor
Deb Miner, series designer
Ciara Beitlich, book designer
Bridget Prehn, photo researcher

Photos by iStock/Valerii Evlakhov cover,
16; Alamy/Helmut Cornel 1; Alamy/
Stephen Frink Collection 3; Minden/
Sergio Hanquet 4-5; Alamy/Jesse
Cancelmo 6-7; Shutterstock/Eric Isselee
8-9; Alamy/Nature Picture Library
10-11; Alamy/Reinhard Dirscherl 12-13;
Getty/Gallo Images 14-15

EELS